The new and complete guide 2016.
Guide from first-person, based on personal experience.
Very handy and informative guide.

Includes all the necessary links for easy moving, routes and lots of useful information.
This guide includes the Top 100 best places where You can exciting to spend your vacation in Iceland.
Here You will find essential information for planning Your rest.
Attractions such as:
Spa Blue Lagoon;
Geysers;

Waterfalls;

Glaciers

National parks and others.

Places where you can interesting and fun to spend your time.
With this guide, you can easily choose a place for
accommodation.
Hotels, shops, night clubs, and many outdoor activities such
as:
Whale watching

Diving

Surfing,

Mountain safaris,

Ice climbing

Salmon fishing,

Horse riding, and others.

Also here You will find lots of useful information, such as where to buy unlimited 4G Internet across the country. The best and most interesting route, step-by-step throughout Iceland. Information on how to reach, where to stay and weather conditions will help You better plan your trip. In this guide You will not have to re-read lots of "guff", it's just the facts and specifics".

PS I Hope my guide will be useful for You and You will enjoy Your trip in full.

CONTENT

CHAPTER 1

GENERAL FACTS ABOUT THE ICELAND.

Travel to Iceland can be compared to a walk on the Moon or Mars, everything here is unusual and fantastic.

Iceland is a large island in the North Atlantic. Here live the descendants of the Vikings. This country is the westernmost country in Europe with the northernmost capital of the world.

For the first time seeing the Icelandic landscape, you can imagine yourself Neil Armstrong first stepping on the moon – his whole horizon covered with fancy solidified lava, craters, imposing basalt cliffs and colorful rhyolite mountains. Stone beauty is replaced by wide meadows, kind of reminds of a scene from Lord of the rings.

Complete the picture of Iceland nature hot mineral water geysers splashing from the ground. Grand waterfalls, fog, and dew beautifully settles on the rocks and grass around the geysers.

The trip to Iceland will allow you to access a world in which people still live, surrounded by wild and beautiful Nordic nature, but their level of living standard is one of the best in the world.

Pristine untouched nature will delight you: huge glaciers, volcanoes, powerful waterfalls, and hot springs. The country is rich in traditions - houses of the Icelanders, their music, history - all is full of national flavor. This island will give you energy and amazing nature, colorful and vivid will leave an unforgettable experience.

WEATHER IN ICELAND THROUGHOUT ON YEAR

In Iceland you can go in summer and winter you will always find many interesting things on this island. Weather here is harsh but fresh air like here is hard to find somewhere else.

Iceland weather in summer warmer, softer and the wind is blowing here not so much.

Due to volcanic activity, numerous geysers and hot springs, the island is always warming up and the air temperature in the coldest months in winter does not fall below 25-27 ^{0}F (– 3 – 4 ^{0}C). In winter, the air in Iceland becomes even purer and more transparent.

Summer in Iceland

The second half of May and until the end of July in Iceland, the daylight 24 hours a day. At the end of June in Reykjavik, the sun sinks beneath the horizon less than 3 hours. Walking at midnight in the city, completely forget about time, about that night now. And although there is no sunlight, but the sky is still bright and blue as the day.

The hottest summer month is July, when average daytime temperatures remain in the range of 57-59 ^{0}F (14-15 ^{0}C) and night 44-50 ^{0}F (7-10 ^{0}C). In summer the weather is changing warm, cool and wet periods. From June to August, Iceland offers the most for travel, middle of summer here – the warm, when the temperatures reach 68 ^{0}F (20 ^{0}C). In August, in Iceland the average temperature is around 59 ^{0}F (15 ^{0}C).

Autumn in Iceland

In October the weather changes highly, this is due to cyclones which pass through the Atlantic Ocean.

As for November, this time begins a dark period when the weather in Iceland in the fall depends on the height of the Sun.

Winter in Iceland

In the winter in all of Iceland common cold strong wind. In December comes the dark season when daylight lasts more than five hours. In General, the weather in Iceland in winter is mild and windy. The coldest month of the winter season – January, this time on the coast the temperature during the day is from 32-35 ^{0}F (0 to 2 ^{0}C), and at night: 25-27 ^{0}F (– 3 – 4 ^{0}C).

Spring off the coast of Iceland accumulates drift ice, which begins to gather in the winter. Because in March in Iceland the temperature remains in the range of 35-37 ^{0}F (2-3 ^{0}C) and begins to decrease the amount of precipitation. But the weather in Iceland in the spring remains of the snow, just snow at this time is not as active as in winter. In April and may in Iceland is getting warmer and temperatures rise to around 44-50 ^{0}F (7-10 ^{0}C).

Actual weather in Iceland you can always find on the weather site
http://www.vedur.is

CHAPTER 2. HOW TO GET TO ICELAND

In Iceland you can get two ways, by air and by sea. Flights from the USA will take 4-6 hours. Flight from Europe will take 3-4 hours. Additionally, you can make a short trip to Atlantic if you choose tour by ferry.

In Iceland there are no railways. If you would like to travel to Iceland without a car, you can move easily around the country on buses. The bus service developed here is well.

FLY TO ICELAND

If you choose air travel, you arrive in the Keflavik International Airport, also known as Reykjavik-Keflavik Airport (KEF). The airport is located 30 miles (50km) from the capital of Iceland, Reykjavik.

You can stay in Keflavik and start your journey from this city or you can travel to Reykjavik in a rented car on the road 41, take a taxi or bus transfer.

Bus tickets can be purchased online or to pay on the spot. In the arrivals hall are located the offices of the major carriers: Airport Express and FlyBus. Buses expect arrived tourists opposite the exit from airport. Buses go after 30-40 minutes after the arrival of each new flight.

You can book your transfer from the airport on the airportexpress or flybus a one-way ticket costs 20-25$. Travel time is 45 min.

Taxi price from the airport to Reykjavik is about 120$

If you plan to travel around Iceland by bus, buy a bus card. It will save your travel budget.
You also can order a bus card

BOOK AIR TICKETS
You can book tickets for flights on the website of the Icelandic international airlines Icelandair
This airline operates flights to Iceland from most American cities.
Also you can pick and book air tickets from another carrier, for example: Wowair, Delta, Easyjet

SAIL TO ICELAND
Another way to get to Iceland is by ferry from the Danish port of Hirtshals are both. The ship overcomes the Atlantic in 2 days, and return trip for 2 people with passenger cars will cost an approximate 4000$ without a meal on Board. But this way you can travel around Iceland by car.

You can book your ferry crossing through online booking engine

http://www.smyrilline.com/

CHAPTER 3. WHERE TO STAY WHILE TRAVELLING IN ICELAND

CAMPING'S

If you choose campsites for an overnight stay in Iceland you have many choices for accommodation.

In Iceland officially registered about 70 campsites. Campsites located along the main road No. 1, in remote mountainous areas and in the fjords. Campgrounds are open from May to September. The average daily cost per person is $10.

The first campground where you can stay iStay is 5 miles from Keflavik international airport to Sandgerdi, southern Peninsula, on the street Byggdavegur Reykjavik is 35 miles away. If you choose this campground to stop, remember, just 18 miles away is the famous Bluelagoon.

Another campsite called T-baer is located in the bay of Herdisarvik in 33 miles from Reykjavik. To reach this campsite from Keflavik international airport, head South-East on 41st road, then South on 43 and turn East on road 427.

Near the village of Vik, you'll be able to settle in Vikcamping which takes guests from June until late September.

In the East of Iceland you can stay in camping Mjoifjordur. The Eastern fjords are very beautiful and you will be able to travel the East coast quite a lot of time, there is always something to see and to do.

Lonsa is a comfortable camping place outside Akureyri.

All campsites close at the end of September.

HOSTEL'S

In Iceland capital you can stay in Reykjavik city hostel

Two, three and six-bedded rooms each have a shower. This hostel has a comfortable courtyard with its garden.

Free Internet access, equipped kitchen and Laundry facilities. Everything you need. You can free to store your Luggage and use of household appliances, computer.

The reception is open 24 hours.

Nearby there is located 24-hours supermarket.

In the village of Vik is a cozy hostel which offers a wonderful view. Everything you need is here to stay. Here is beautiful nature, south shore and a large black beach. Here is a nice quiet rest, tourists like hiking. Nearby you can play golf, go horse riding or boating in the sea.

Hofn is a small town with three sides washed by the sea and on the fourth side is covered by the largest glacier Vatnajokull.

The hostel is located in the city center and everything you need is at your fingertips.

Staying in Hofn you will always find something to do, boat tours, glacier walks on horses, snowmobiles or jeeps. Here you will not be bored.

In the East of Iceland you can stay in town Seydisfjordur

Hostel in Seydisfjordur is located in a former harbor, and the reception is next to the building of the old hospital. Both buildings have a long history and not long been renovated. The hostel is located just a few hundred yards from the center. Cozy two – six bedded rooms are decorated with antique furniture. Beautiful views of the fjord it looks from the hostel.

Internet connection and home appliances are available at this hostel. There is always you will be happy.

In the Northern capital of Iceland, the city of Akureyri hostel is located in the city center. This hostel owned by the same family for over 50 years. The hostel has a common room, kitchen and dining room. Cozy rooms with bathrooms and shower. As there is a separate cottage with all amenities. In Akureyri you will find many interesting tours such us whale watching, or for example skiing on the glacier etc.

GUEST HOUSES

If you like more comfort, then choose the guesthouses or hotels.

In Iceland, quite a lot of guesthouses. This is a cozy home that is less than hotels and sometimes have only one or two rooms for settlement. Often the guesthouse manages the Icelandic family. Therefore, you will be taken with maximum care. In the guesthouse there are all the amenities, shower, food, internet. In most of the guesthouses offer free breakfast.

Some excellent Guest Houses in Iceland:

In the Reykjavik
https://www.facebook.com/Reykjavik.City.Hostel/
In the South http://www.hostel.is/Hostels/Vik
In the East http://www.hostel.is/Hostels/Seydisfjordur/
In the North http://www.hostel.is/Hostels/Akureyri/

HOTELS

The network of hotels "Edda" includes 11 hotels located around the coast of Iceland (the route of the Golden Ring). Hotels can offer You many different services such as:
rent of transport, open pools with thermal water, conference rooms, restaurants, geothermal baths, kayaks and pleasure boats, various excursions, fishing, golf, horse riding, gyms, also whale watching and birds in their natural environment and of course not forgetting the magnificent landscapes.

Also in network hotels "Edda", hosts various events like The Great Fish Day or a music concert's.

By staying in a hotel Edda You will be satisfied by spending the holiday and get a lot of impressions.

CHAPTER 4. HOW TO SPEND YOUR REST IN ICELAND

WHALE WATCHING

Around the coast of Iceland, it is often possible to meet and observe some of the largest mammals of the world:

whales, sharks, sperm whales, blue whales and many other inhabitants of the Atlantic Ocean.

One of favorite pastime of tourists in Iceland is whale watching. If you are interested, go to the North of the country – that is where the best place for a meeting with the ocean residents.

In the North, on the Bay of Skjalfandi is a small and very charming town of Husavik, which is the largest in Europe center, whale watching.

- Whaaaale! - shouted the captain, pointing to the front. With delight and anticipation, run to the Board and see the fountain of the whale. This fountain gushes out water at 32.8 - 16,4 yards from you, and you imagine the animal 39,3-45,9 ft in length, slowly moving under water.

Suddenly, the captain shouts, "He's diving!", Whale flexes and arch its back, raising huge tail and disappears again, plunging into the depths. All accompanied by the enthusiastic cries of the children, clicking cameras and applause of the international public.

Whales spark emotional reactions in just about everyone. Mostly it is the whales become a metaphor for the natural balance on Earth. Sperm whales are superior to all the world's mammals in diving. They can dive to a depth of 328 yards, so you are unlikely to see twice the same whale in one trip. But, the chance to see several whales are very large, as the safaris are arranged in areas rich in fish, plankton and crustaceans. Here for food sail thousands of whales.

In the summer you can often see sperm whales, but if you are lucky, you can also look at the toothed whales, sharks, blue whales, moor whales, humpback whales, dolphins and orcas. In addition, whale Safari you will have amazing scenery of Iceland, the abundance of fresh sea air and beauty that will long stay with you!

Duration: 3 -3.5 hours

NORTHERN LIGHTS

October in Iceland began tours for those wishing to experience the Northern lights. One of the most interesting programs are offered in the southern part of the country. First, tourists are taken to the town of Stokkseyri, there are many stories about elves and ghosts. There is Icelandic Wonders Center and Icelandic wonders dedicated to elves, trolls and Northern lights.

In the "winter" part of the Icelandic Wonders Center, where it is maintained at subzero temperatures, watching a movie about the Northern lights, tourists are offered to enjoy a drink, ice, which gouged out Europe's largest glacier Vatnajokull. Then tourists are taken to Draugasetrid ("Center of ghosts"), where the mazes are told and played back 24 scary stories. After that begins the hunt for the Northern lights.

Conscientious travel agencies arrange (such) tours Northern lights with professional "hunter". Best of all it is a unique natural phenomenon can be seen in the period from 22:00 to midnight. Thus, while tourists enjoy evening cultural program and refreshments, a professional "hunter" rides in the surrounding area and looking for a place where best to observe the Northern lights. Only after the lights has been found, the "hunter" (is associated with the guide and) call the whole group to the specified place.

Northern lights – a phenomenon that attracts and amazes people for centuries. Celestial patterns, changing every second, in fact, are only the result of the collision of the solar wind with the Earth's atmosphere. This process goes continuously, and therefore, theoretically, the Northern lights occur year round, however it is not visible always. The best place to observe this miracle of nature – the Arctic, but the best time is from October to March, this is the darkest time of the year and are therefore less likely to see the Northern lights increases. Besides dark, it is important that the sky was clear: even a small cloud will prevent the clear glow of the Northern lights.

GEOTHERMAL POOLS AND SPAS

Geothermal Blue Lagoon, formed around a set of natural pools, is one of the most popular natural attractions of Iceland. Every year the resort is visited by **almost** 300 thousand people. **The first** bathing area appeared in the Blue lagoon in the mid 80-ies of the last century. Hot springs sky blue, baby blue and milk shades is washed by the lava piles, creating contrasting landscapes.

Known since 1976 volcanic origin complex has a unique therapeutic and healing properties. Minerals, sea salt, sulphur and blue-green algae in water can cure skin diseases. Swimming here even in winter: water in deep tanks throughout the year, retains a comfortable temperature from +37°to +40°C.

WORKING HOURS

The blue lagoon is open daily throughout the year. Working hours in June: from 9:00 to 21:00; from July 1 to August 15: from 9:00 to midnight, from August 16 to 30: from 9:00 to 21:00 from September 1 to May 31: from 10:00 to 20:00. With the exception of Christmas and New Year holidays; during the period from 23 December to 1 January, the schedule should specify on Bluelagoon official site. Guests can stay in the thermal complex for 45 minutes after closing.

THE COST OF ATTENDING

The price of admission depends on the season. From September 1 to may 31 the cost of visiting the Blue Lagoon is 33 euros for adults, 15 euros for teenagers 14 and 15 years. From 1 June to 31 August entrance for adults will cost 40 euros, for teenagers 14 and 15 years - 15 euros. For children under 13 enter for free when accompanied by adults.

More information about the cost of cosmetic procedures, as well as rental of bath robes and towels can be found on the website of Blue Lagoon.

TIPS

All visitors to the Blue Lagoon resort will receive a bracelet with a magnetic chip that is the key to a personal locker. You need to bring swimsuit, towels and bathrobes can be rented for an additional fee. Locker rooms are divided into male and female areas. There are showers (shampoo and shower gel are provided free of charge). Also a bracelet with a chip is used to pay for snacks and drinks in the bar and restaurant, thermal baths, so that the money and other things best left in the locker.

To visit the Blue lagoon special shoes not required

The water in the pools is renewed every two days.

On the Blue Lagoon website has a special section where you can consult or ask question about features of the resort.

HOW TO GET

Geothermal Blue Lagoon is located 23.6 miles to the South-West of Reykjavik; travel time from capital bus station is 45 minutes. To reach the resort as you can from Keflavik international airport, located 9.3 miles North West from the Blue Lagoon.Travel time - about twenty minutes. Buses run between Reykjavik, airport and thermal baths several times a day throughout the year.

The resort has free lockers where you can leave suitcases and bags.

LOCATION

Geothermal Blue Lagoon is on Reykjanes Peninsula in southwest Iceland. GPS 63°52'53.4" N22°27'10.1"W

ACTIVE HOLIDAYS IN ICELAND

DIVING

Although it is accepted that diving and snorkeling are engaged in tropical latitudes, where there are exotic fish, the icy waters around Iceland will amaze you with its transparency. Also you can enjoy a breathtaking sight born of the earth's crust on a fault Mid-Atlantic ridge.

HORSE RIDING

What could be better than to admire the scenery of Iceland, sitting on horseback? Although Icelandic horses are slightly less than we are used to, call them ponies would be a mistake. They have two additional gaits that makes the ride very special.

CAVING

Corridors of lava and caves in Iceland can be found at every step. A small entrance on the surface often results in huge caves where you will see unique geological formations – stalagmites and stalactites.

KAYAKING

Icelandic clear river ideal for kayaking and rafting on quiet secluded fjords – with what incomparable pleasure.

Rafting If you are not afraid of ice water, then rafting Iceland for you. And if you're bored of the simply rapids overcoming, you can always try out rafting.

ICE CLIMBING

The Glaciers are constantly melting and moving, every day changing their shape, but you will always find a vertical wall of ice. Tour operators offer full year trips for ice climbers of all skill levels.

HIKING

In the mountains of Iceland you will find great **routes** for every taste: from short walks to multi-day hikes. For example, in the Park of Skaftafell, which is part of the largest national Park, Vatnajokull, you will see sharp mountain peaks, shining snow caps and barren plains, sloping down to the shore.

SNOWMOBILES

Snowmobile is a kind of alternative to Hiking: less energy, but just as exciting way to experience the Icelandic glaciers.

MOUNTAIN SAFARI

The Harsh Icelandic highlands covered with snow. But on jeeps you can explore the mountains at any time of the year.

SURFING

In recent years Iceland has gained a reputation as one of the best places for surfing. Though the low water temperature you can conquer the great waves here. You just need especially tight suit. In Iceland there are a few surfers who go to sea all year round and visitors can always contact the tour operators.

SALMON FISHING

Icelandic rivers are rich in salmon, so the most famous fishermen are happy to come to Iceland to throw their fishing rods.

CHAPTER 5. CAPITAL REYKJAVIK

THE SIGHTS OF REYKJAVIK

BEACH NAUTHOLSVIK

Guests of Reykjavik has long been appreciated yacht club "Siglunes" and the geothermal beach in Nautholsvik.

High mineralization of geothermal water helps to get rid of many chronic diseases and enhances immunity.

On-site: service center with locker rooms, showers, hot baths and a wide selection of beverages. Optimum temperature of the seawater lagoon is holding at 15-19 °C, the bath is brought to 30-39 °C.

Yacht club "Siglunes" is located on the East side geothermal beach and children the opportunity to spend unforgettable sailing holidays.

In contrast to the comfortable Spa centers, beach Nautholsvik in a public place, and therefore sometimes crowded. Nothing surprising, because the view is stunning and plus, this is probably the only place where you can really "touch" the boundary between the hot thermal water and the freezing breath of the ocean.

MUSEUM OF PHOTOGRAPHY

5 million items were collected at the photography Museum of Reykjavik. In this unique archive are the various collections of photos taken by both professionals and Amateurs. The oldest photo is dated 1870

Topics variety from cute family pictures to industrial landscapes. On each slice of life. The whole history of Iceland: its customs and way of life, traditions, industrial development, fashion, advertising, natural beauty. There are pictures that are forever kept in memory of the disappeared under the onslaught of civilization the wonders of the world. Exhibitions are regularly changed and updated.

Very original entertainment invented in the Museum of photography for young visitors. They made miniature camera, similar to the houses. It is both a space for games and at the same time a small exhibition of photographs. Children can feel inside the camera, touch everything is inside this mysterious chamber, to see how it turns out the.

LAKE ELLIDAVATN

One of the greatest advantages of Reykjavik is that you never, even being in the capital, will not be divorced from nature. Lake Ellidavatn is just a 15-minute drive from the city center and is a fantastic way to dive into the past.

Ellidavatn is popular not just of excellent fishing, and also good climate which positively influences health. Lake water full of fish, in the first this is silver trout and fat salmon.

Fishing is permitted daily from 7 am to midnight, and the season for fans to sit with a fishing rod begins with the first day of summer and ends on September 15. Especially popular lake in late may – early June, and the best chance to pick up on the hook the trout closer to the evening or early morning. Despite that the here always welcome to fishermen, the rules are strict, the population of valuable fish is under special control.

Large penalties for abandoned garbage on the shore, ride only on strictly paved route, navigation is prohibited without special permission. Moreover all anglers must write a report on their catch on a special website.

FJORD, HVALFJORDUR

Once out of the Reykjavik and go past the adjacent town of Mosfellsbaer, the circular road will lead you to the North, where the towering mountain ash., This Fjord, Hvalfjordur, which means "whale fjord". The biggest in southwest Iceland, named after the huge number of whales, the legends of which go with the times of the first settlers.

In this area there are many interesting tourist routes. One of them is in Thingvellir national Park.
Fjord Hvalfjordur has always been one of the main whaling stations in Iceland.

Water of the fjord teeming with fish, this is where the main migration routes of herring river full of salmon.

SPA-CENTER "BLUE LAGOON"

Blue lagoon Iceland is a dream of everyone who wants not just to relax, but feel renewed and emerged, in the truest sense of the word, from a geothermal source. This Spa the most, today visited attraction in Iceland. The resort is located in the South-West of the country, in Grindavik, at 40 minutes drive from Reykjavik and a short distance from Keflavik airport.

The main treatment in the "Blue lagoon" is carried out by using mineral water, which is very rich in beneficial substances, in its composition silica and sulfur. The waters of the lagoon are renewed every two days, due to the plant geothermal energy. Services that are offered, unique, there are few centers in the world who have such a generous natural base. At the services of visitors (as) a medical center and a beauty salon. You can choose everything that your heart desires. It can be a relaxing massage using special oil with a active minerals. The skin becomes healthy and glowing.

In the composition of the scrub local cooking silica lagoon, which resurfaces the skin, removes dead cells and stimulates circulation. All cosmetics used in the Spa "Blue lagoon" is prepared based on the geothermal seawater, minerals and algae. Cosmetics with such a composition can be found only in Iceland. Very popular amongst the guests of the center, treatments with algae. Professionals can polish the skin with special body wraps. Developed in "the Blue lagoon" the whole system is the strengthening of procedures for pregnant women that relieves swelling and pain in the back.

Beauty- it's a true care for face and body. Special cream and massage make the skin more elastic and visibly reduce the signs of aging. Facials are divided into three categories, each designed for different skin types. For Mature skin, they are directed to their own production of collagen and provide essential moisture. For normal and dry, it's first and foremost the strengthening of the protective barrier. Dry and mixed skin, it's subjected to deep purification and detoxification. Very effective deep cleansing mask-based of silica

Also available VIP-service in spa-center. Exclusive interior, which implies privacy and quiet. This complex is designed for 12 people maximum. Living room with fireplace and designer furniture, it's an oasis separated from the bustle. Direct individual access to the therapeutic waters of the lagoon is provided for guests. In addition to relaxing Spa treatments, guests are awaited and exciting excursion. Experienced guides tell the history of the resort with the natural features of this place, and its value from the point of view of medical science. Everyone can visit the lava fields that stretched near to the Spa and learn a lot about volcanic activity in Iceland. The tour necessarily include local myths about elves and trolls, as well as a original cocktail "Blue lagoon", visit laboratories and a little surprise.

GEYSIR "GREAT GEYSIR"

The route "the Golden ring" is the famous Valley of geysers. Among a dozen large and small sources guides pay attention to the oldest and most famous of them –the Great Geysir. Received its name in the mid-thirteenth century from the Icelandic word "geyser", which means "to break", he gave the name to all other hot springs in the world.

Great Geysir was born after the earthquake in 1294. As a result of the cracking of the earth's crust opened the hot springs under the ground. With a hiss escaping to the outside, they began to gush to a height of about 70 meters. The spectacle is quite fascinating and still attracts crowds of tourists. This geyser wakes up and dies down periodically, and always it is associated with volcanic activity. The diameter of the Geysir is about 3 meters. It's a huge bowl, composed of small limestone rock. During the eruption, he throws up about 230 tons of water!

THE HISTORY OF THE GEYSER

In the history of the well preserved facts Geysir's life over the last two centuries. In 1894, a local farmer who owned the land in the Valley of geysers, sold it to businessman

James Kreiger (by the way, later he became head of the Northern Ireland government). The new owner fenced it and did the entrance fee. Some time later gave (!) this unique area to his friend.

In 1935, one of the descendants of the owner sells the land with geysers to Sigurdur Jonasson. Driven by the best motives, that makes the area a national treasure and made the free entrance. But as known, "The road to hell is paved with good intentions". Thanks to the free access to the natural wonder some cultureless people ... it was very interesting to throw rocks and dried dirt in a geyser. Spouting of geyser was ended.

It was necessary to save this important touristic area. At the governmental level was made a decision to create an artificial canal around the geyser, to forcing it work. But these measures gave short-term effect. Currently, the canals are artificially washed, before the main holiday of Iceland – the Day of national Independence. In 2000, was a huge earthquake in Iceland. Obviously, the channels of the main geyser was cleaned by natural way.

Geyser have been operated again in active mode: the eruption took place up to 8 times a day, however, the water fountain was low. But this activity has gone too on recession after three years. Now the Great Geysir "wakes up" rarely spouting not more than 10 meters. Its main condition – the tranquil lake of turquoise color with a smell of hydrogen sulfide. To attract more tourists in the Valley of geysers well-developed infrastructure. There's a hotel, café and restaurant, in a souvenir shop you can buy models of geysers, and utensils and summer clothes with their image.

There are stamps, commemorative coins, on which are emblazoned the Great Geysir. The guards keep order in the tourist groups. Eruption of thermal springs associated with the high temperature water. If you do not follow precautions, you can get burned. By the way, a lot of unwary animals killed them and cooked alive. But there are swimming areas where the water isn't hot..

By the way, Reykjavik is heated by hot spring water. Due to the cheapness of this fuel, the Icelanders can afford to grow of exotic flowers, fruit and vegetables in numerous greenhouses.

PEACE TOWER

On the Videy island in Iceland located a place called the Peace Tower. This tower brings wisdom, healing and joy. Light beam that penetrate the heavens – it's meant to show peace and love – primary thing that binds and sustains life on Earth. Peace tower, also called the Tower of Light it's a memorial to John Lennon , built by his widow Yoko Ono in 2007. This is a huge 17 meters in diameter pedestal of white stone.

Approximately on 24 languages of the world are inscribed the famous words from the song " Imagine peace." The tower it's an illusion, created by bright beams of light directed into the sky. The light rays out of the cylinders, embedded in a stone base. When the weather is clear, the height of rays can be up to 4 kilometers.

The build of Peace Tower started on 9 October 2007, the birthday of the famous musician. One year later the first ray of light has illuminated the heaven. Yoko has developed the design of the tower by herself. At the opening she said that this tower was the embodiment of their shared husband dreams. "I chose Iceland, because the Peace Tower should stand in a unique clean place. Every time I visit this place, it makes me feel 10 years younger. This is actually an answer to prayer for me because the first time John has put forward this idea at home, in England, in 1966.

Lennon didn't knew how to realize this a project and was intend to build a lighthouse in his garden. I never thought that this could be a reality." Tower on the island of Videy should remind people that the world need to be protected. Because the tower and all the inscriptions on the pedestal is a reminder of the peace hymn which was written by John Lennon – "Imagine". Iceland is difficult to surprise with light show. This country has numerous volcanic eruptions, the bright flashes of the Northern lights...

However, in this enlightened country I've never seen anything that would compete with a brilliant trace of light that the penetrated the darkness of the Arctic at night of October 9, at night, when John Lennon would have turned 67 years old. In the presence of 200 people, including Yoko Ono, Sean Lennon (John's son), Ringo Starr, Olivia, widow of George Harrison, and prominent companions of the Dalai Lama, together with the civilian leaders of the city of Reykjavik, the Tower of peace was turned on for the first time..

The light, on the Videy island, switched on at October 9, John Lennon's birthday and it's lit until 8 December, the date when he was murdered. At this day, the lights go out. Also floodlights shine on special occasions. The tower illuminated in winter solstice (21st to 28th December), New Year's eve (31 December) and the first week of the Icelandic spring (from 21 to 28 March). It lights up after sunset, two hours before midnight.

HARPA CONCERT HALL

Concert hall Harpa in Reykjavik's harbor is the most beautiful place in Iceland for a concerts, business meetings, large conferences, banquets and exhibitions. Its vivid facade designed by renowned artist and architect Olafur Eliasson. He drew inspiration from crystallizing basalt columns commonly found in Icelandic nature.

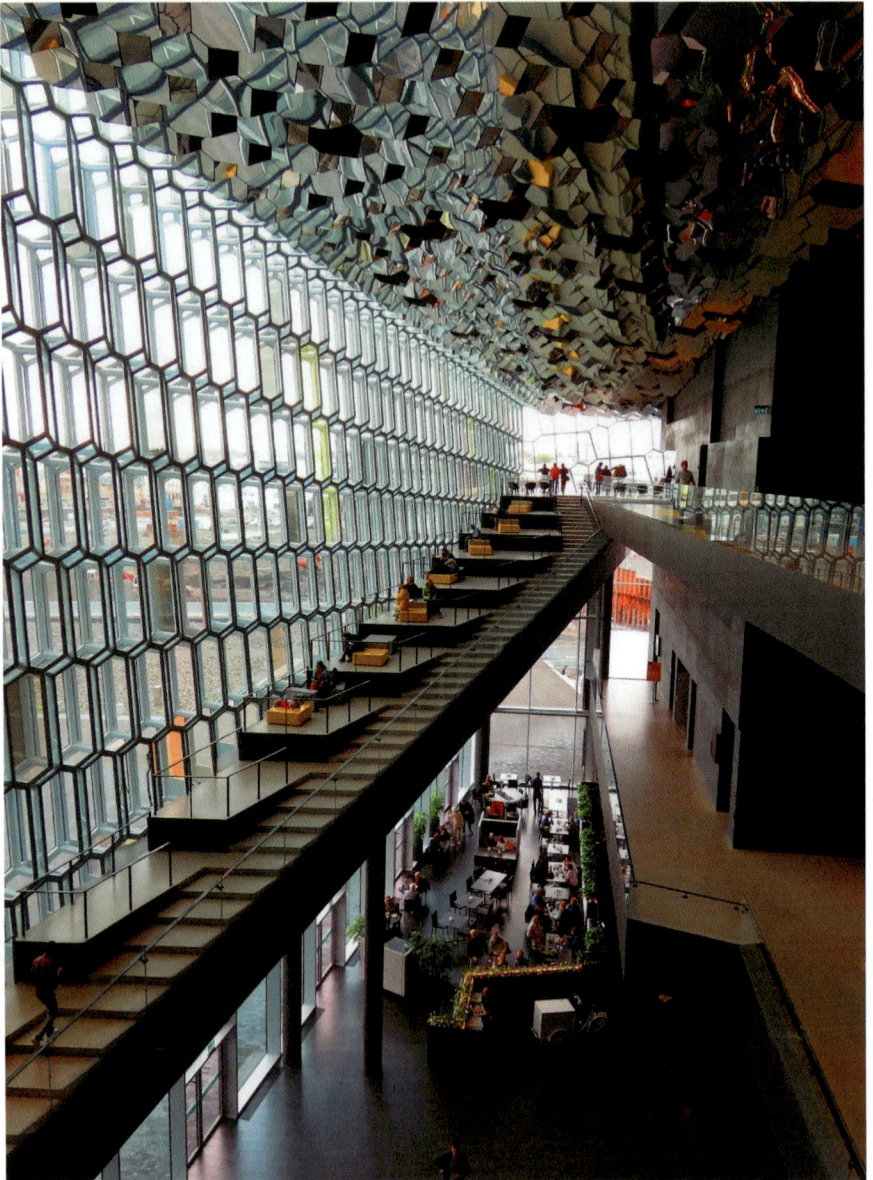

The strategic geographical position of Iceland, right in the middle of transatlantic routes, making it an optimal place for meetings on neutral territory – only a 3 hour flight from London and 5 hours from New York. Business and creative teams arriving from Europe or North America, always glad to choose exotic Iceland, country with one of the fastest growing tourism sector. And the most important meetings always held in the hall Harpa.

Solid glass wall of the facade changes color depending on the movement of the sun and weather changes.

In 2011, the concert hall became the permanent home for the Icelandic Symphony orchestra. They gives up to 60 concerts each season. Many of the most famous musicians in the world come from this team, including Daniel Barenboim, Anne-Sophie mutter, Joshua bell, Hilary Hahn, Mstislav Rostropovich, Radu Lupu, Claudio Arrau, and Evelyn Glennie.

ZOOLOGICAL FAMILY PARK

On 22 April 1986 the City Council of Reykjavik made a decision of construction of the ZOO in which the main will be farm animals and wild native species.

When the first settlers arrived in Iceland every animal in addition to foxes doesn't lived in these parts.

All other types were imported and adapted to local conditions. Cows were brought from England, France and Norway, the goats arrived with the first inhabitants. Now, centuries later an Icelandic sheep's is just a huge demand in the US and Canada, pigeons bred for aesthetic purposes. The history of each breed can be found in the zoo.

The main inhabitants of the Park: horses, sheep, goats, foxes, cattle, pigs, minks, deer's, seals, hens, turkeys, pigeons, rabbits, Guinea pigs, geese, ducks, dogs and cats. In the Park are constantly on the treatment of wild birds. Zoo has grown in this country. Getting acquainted with farm animals you can feel like a farmer: to milk cows, to cut the sheep, feed the hens. In recreation places guests can play games, relax, go cycling, horseback riding etc.

MANSION HOFDI HOUSE

The Ministry of foreign Affairs of Iceland, has officially stated "We can not confirm or deny the information that in the house lives a Ghost." But one of the British diplomats, Greenaway John, which lived for a long-time in a beautiful mansion in Iceland, claimed, that he saw he ghost of the young woman every night in the house.

Moreover, the diplomat convinced the authorities to refuse using the mansion as a dwelling for the consuls. As a consequence, in 1952 government of Iceland became the house owner, since it's used for official receptions and meetings of the municipality. Among the most renowned guests of the Hofdi-house mansion – the king of Norway, presidents of France and Italy, the Queen of England and Denmark, Chancellor Willy Brandt of Germany, and many well-known politicians.

But, of course, the most historically important meeting was held at the Hofdi house in 1986, between U.S. President Ronald Reagan and Soviet Union head Mikhail Gorbachev. This meeting effectively ended the cold war. In memory of the meeting in the building hung the flags of the USA and the USSR. The old-timers say that the house is built on an ancient burial ground of Vikings.

VIKIN MARITIME MUSEUM

Welcome to the Museum at the seafront. The Iceland's history, present and future are closely connected with seafaring. This activity determines the character of the nation, it is difficult to understand this country without knowing its Maritime history. Exhibitions of the Vikin Maritime Museum allow you to look at the relationship of Iceland to the sea for centuries, they illustrate the development of the fleet from rowing boats to modern trawlers and powerful cargo ships.

The main highlight of the Museum is "Odinn". It's a legendary ship. He was the best patrol and rescue vessel, almost 200 ships in distress was towed to a safe place. Coast guard vessel was built in Aalborg in Denmark in 1959. It has a displacement of 910 tons, length 63 m, a specially reinforced hull for navigation in ice. His most powerful weapon – 57mm gun located on the nose. Vikin maritime Museum have a fun gift shop. There you can find a lot of interesting items, very bright with an Icelandic twist: Souvenirs, toys, books for children and adults, CD's with Icelandic folk music. The Museum works full year.

ICELANDIC PHALLOLOGICAL MUSEUM

The Icelandic phallus Museum, founded in 1997, a former teacher Sigurdur Hardarson. For 37 years he taught history and Spanish at Reykjavík. His unusual hobby started in childhood, after he received in a gift of a whip made from a bull penis.

Hardarson started collecting exhibits around the country. Their sizes are from 2 mm. to 170 see. Phallus of a blue whale or a phallus of the hamster, which can only be seen through a magnifying glass. Many of the exhibits, supplied by local fishermen. In slaughterhouse Hardarsson got the bodies of farm animals. After commercial whaling was banned, the owner of the Museum began its own hunt for the phallus. He took the bodies of died large animals that ashore to cast.

The penis of a polar bear was received from the hunters who was shot the animal, drifting on an ice floe. Big money was paid for sex organ of elephant, the length of which is almost a meter. The Museum has penises of all mammals which live in Iceland. In addition, the exhibition features many items of phallic art, such as the lampshade made of the scrotum of the bull, the engraving depicting the circumcision of Christ. All around decorated with carved wooden penises

All phalluses are stored in formaldehyde or dried and hanging on the walls. From a particularly large bull penis was maded a cane. In the preparing collection, Charterstone helps his family, though not without embarrassment. He considers himself a true enthusiast and says that in the pursuit of these bodies we can't stop, you can always find a better than the previous exhibit. Originally the collection was housed in the office of Sigurdur Thorarinsson, but after he retired he had the idea to put the exhibits on public display. For this purpose he received a grant from City Council

German collector wanted to buy this collection, but Hardarson refused, explaining that it's unique and should be in his home country. The Museum has become popular with tourists, most of them women. In addition, the Museum argued that the showpieces of folklore section is nothing like the phalluses of trolls and elves and the one-eyed monsters. Sigurdur said that the penis of the elf, which described in museum catalog as "big and old", is one of his favorites.

55 whale penises, 36 of seals and 118 penises of various mammals, and one penis that belonged to a man. The long-awaited donor organ Museum received in June 2011, but this showpiece was received after traumatic amputation, and therefore represents a gray-brown wrinkled mass in a jar of formaldehyde. Therefore, the proposal of the Museum to purchase the "fresh" exhibit is still valid.

NIGHT LIFE. 10 NIGHTCLUBS AND DISCOS OF REYKJAVIK

Night "cream" for the young people in Iceland are available in one place — in a nightclub "Bohem". This location is a kind of mix between a bar, a restaurant and a club, but that's what makes Bohem is so popular. Here are lovely girls on the stage, which can stir up the crowd of dancing, meanwhile, bartenders, skillfully manipulated behind the counter, one after the other serves delicious drinks and cocktails at reasonable cost that's available to everyone.

Address: Grensasvegur 7, Reykjavik

Phone: 354-517-3530

Elegant, uniquely decorated rooms Vegamot daily greeted visitors who want to enjoy a delicacies of Icelandic cuisine. At night this place is transformed and becomes one of the night clubs in the city. Everyone: famous singers, politicians, tourists, and ordinary citizens who searching for fun, great music, great show and just perfect service all of them have choosen this club for this.

Address: Vegamotastig 4, Reykjavik

Phone: 354-511-3040

Maybe a night club Nasa not to compare, for example, with dance floors of Ibiza, but unlikely to find the best place in Iceland. Performance of top-rated bands of Iceland here the same pattern as the regular music festivals that attract huge number of participants not only from Iceland but from other European countries. Jazz festival and the days of hardcore — just some of them.

Address: Austurvollur square, Reykjavik

Phone: 354-511-1313

In a nightclub Astro know what offer to visitors to return them here again. Fiery rhythms of dance music and sexy "Go-Go" girls — this is only a small part of what awaits visitors. Don't forget about the bar, located at the club, because he invites all to enjoy the best drinks, including cocktails, beer, wines, champagne and cognacs.

Address: Austurstraeti 22, Reykjavik

Phone: 354-552-9222

There is no more hot place in the cool Iceland, than a night club "Pravda". Popular mainly among students, this club offers its guests to enjoy the romance of the Northern night, under the sounds of popular dance tracks and hip-hop. Contrary, they will help you relax and fully immerse yourself in the atmosphere of entertainment which in the night club "Pravda" is more than enough.

Address: Austurstraeti 22, Reykjavik

Phone: 354-552-9222

Like most nightlife of Iceland, "Apotek" daily it's a cafe, offering its guests a fun mix of Icelandic and European cuisine with a smoking hot Argentinean grill. . But at night it's a different institution, the door of which burst from just unreal musical rhythms that can lift the mood of anyone. The only thing you need to remember, coming here is about clothes: sneakers and jeans at the "Apotek" are not popular.

Address: Austurstraeti 16 Reykjavik

Phone: 354-575-7900

"Q" combines a nightclub and a bar. It is very convenient coming here in the afternoon, guests can enjoy great drinks and night — join the noisy crowd dancing on the small dance floor. Among the local "Q" Bar is famous as a popular place for the gays, but that doesn't mean that come here are only people with different sexual orientations. Contrary, "Q" will welcome any visitor!

Address: Ingólfsstræti 3, Reykjavik

Phone: 354-578-7868

Cafe, bistro, restaurant, bar and night club — all this charming place "Solon", offering entertainment and recreation for every taste. Night a small dance floor club welcomes all its guests with relaxed rhythms of modern compositions, while the bar located on the ground floor, simply can not accommodate visitors who prefer a quiet conversation over a cocktail, wine or beer instead loud music

Address: Bankastraeti 7a, Reykjavik

Phone: 354-562-3232

Night club "Gaukur A Stong" after its opening in 1983 started to work like pub, during the operation of the ban on beer it's offered their guests a signature cocktail bjorliki consisting of vodka and non-alcoholic beer. Later, the pub was rebuilt, turning it into a hot night club, where play beginners Icelandic performers on weekdays, but on weekends, the audience warms up popular DJs and famous music group.

Address: Tryggvagata 22, Reykjavik

Phone: 354-551-1556

Disco club "22", as a rule, on weekdays behaves pretty quiet. But once the weekend comes, the club is transformed and becomes one of the hottest spots of night life on the city map. Three floors that can accommodate a good restaurant and several well-equipped dance floors. If you need to talk tête-à-tête, it offers beautifully decorated private rooms for VIPs.

Address: Laugavegur 22, Reykjavik

Phone: 354-511-5522

SHOPPING IN REYKJAVIK

Iceland considered as one of the most expensive countries in Europe, but now the difference with other major cities no longer seems so shocking. Quite expensive here food. Need to know where to shop, to save and pleasuring yourself and others in Reykjavik

One of the cheapest food networks in Iceland are considered "Bonus" market's. You can easily recognize them by the logo of a pink piggy-Bank on yellow background. In Reykjavik,store "Bonus" is on the main street – Laugavegur. Not high prices also in the stores "Kronan" and "Kolaportid market" near the bus stop Lækjartorg. On the market you can stock up on everything you need on Saturdays and Sundays until about three in the afternoon.

Most of shops in Iceland are open from Monday to Thursday. Work hours: from 9 to 18, to Friday 9-19, Saturday 10 to 16 hours. Also part of them runs on Sunday, supermarkets open until 8 p.m. Most of the shops accept card payment, but some offer discounts only cash , if ask. If you are a tourist and shop at Iceland, you have the possibility to return the VAT for the purchased goods, if their total value above 4000 ISK (Icelandic kroner) by purchases in one shop.

In the store you have to pay the sum in full and warn the seller that you need a refund of VAT. The seller will give you a special filled form, with a receipt for the purchase. VAT refund provided at the airport in the window "Tax refund". Then supposed to show the goods to customs and ask them to put a stamp on the form. In most stores you can get a brochure "Shopping in Iceland", which shows the current VAT rates and the possibility of a return.

Here is a rough rates... Food: bread – 150-250 ISK, oil – 150 ISK, eggs (10 pieces) – 400-600 ISK, milk will cost you 150 ISK, a cake in the café 250-500 ISK, a glass of wine or beer – 600 – 800 ISK, pizza pizzeria 1500 ISK. Fuel at gas stations will cost approximately 175-190 ISK, and the price of gasoline often change. Liquid dishwashing costs about 700 ISK, and soap dispenser – 250 ISK.

What to buy as a gift in Iceland?

Pay attention to the products from the wool from the Icelandic sheep, it's perfect quality soft wool . Feature of this wool is that it repels water and is very warm, sweaters, hats, gloves are manufactured from this wool. In our days, mainly things made of wool are produced by machines, but if you try, you can find hand-knitted items. The cost of woolen sweaters starts from 8 000 ISK. Products made of sheep wool are very expensive, but they are great in quality. Hats or gloves are approximately 3 000-5 000 ISK.

There are many small shops that sell crafts and handmade goods, porcelain figurines, paintings, glass and jewelry in Reykjavík. Of course, a great gift with a local flavor will be Icelandic folk music you can buy a lot of CDs with ethno-rock, and record world-known Icelandic singers: Björk, Sigur Rós and others.

Designer fashion in Reykjavik presents several interesting boutiques that are worth attention too. For example, sister's Einvera fashion-designers designed clothes under the brand "Kalda". This is a simple and modern style. Address: Laugarvegur 35, 101 reykjavík). Kiosk is a trendy boutique, which is jointly owned 9 designers. Moreover, they work in turns. They offer an interesting range of flowers and materials. Here you'll find a collection of accessories and jewelry.

Like all Icelanders – fashion here is extremely different from any other countries primarily for its unpredictability and the presence of ethnic motifs in avant-garde processing. The cost of products starts from 100-200 euros.

From Iceland also brought a special cheese, and dried fish, however, those delicacies are not for everyone. Immerse yourself in a world of harsh and peculiar Icelandic worldview.

Discount card of Reykjavik:

Upon arriving in Reykjavik do not forget about possibility of acquiring Reykjavik Welcome Card. *With it, you can save your money in many places in the city. For more details you can read the information on this card here.*

CHAPTER 6. TOURS IN ICELAND

You can travel to Iceland by yourself in a rental car or use the services of local guides.

Learn the main routes in this Chapter and it will be easier to plan the optimal route for you.

In addition to this guide, you can download a list of links to all necessary places in your journey: where to stay, where to eat, where to find excursions, rent a car, boat, ATV and more. You can simply follow one of the routes as described below.

Multi-day itineraries around the island, the routes on the West and East fjords, the inland routes, the single-day routes, routes to the lakes, waterfalls, coasts of Iceland.

The route is planned, where and when you can watch the whales and millions of nesting birds that are not afraid of tourists, and where better to swim to the icebergs and where you need to hunt for the Northern lights.

Follow the route description and you will be easy to focus on each aspect of travel.

The routes in this guide will be updated and receive new routes for travel.

TOUR AROUND THE ISLAND

Upon arrival in Iceland you can stay in Reykjavik.

You can choose your preferred accommodation option in CHAPTER 3. WHERE TO STAY WHILE TRAVELLING IN ICELAND

Information about sights, shops and rest in Reykjavik you will find in CHAPTER 5. CAPITAL REYKJAVIK

DAY ONE. From Reykjavik to Vik (115 miles in transit).

See Eyjafjallajokull volcano, visit to Seljalandsfoss and Skogafoss Waterfalls.

Drive from Reykjavik to the South East on road no.1 heading to Vic. After driving 70 miles from the capital, stop off at Seljalandsfoss Waterfall. Let's continue 18 miles to the South and stop at the Skogafoss Waterfall. Until then Vick will remain 20 miles away.

Before Vic you will meet famous, after its eruption in 2010, the volcano Eyjafjallajokull.

In Vic you will be able to eat in a local cafe or restaurant. If you are not travelling in a hurry, we recommend you to stay the night in Vik.

Till evening you will be able to enjoy nature and beautiful scenery, riding along the southern coast of Iceland.

DAY TWO. From Vik to Hofn with a stop in Skaftafell National Park and Ice Lagoon (150 miles in transit).

Leaving Vic on east along road no. 1 to the town of Hof. Here visit Skaftafell (Vatnajokull) desert with geysers and volcanoes in Skaftafell (Vatnajokull) National Park.

20 miles drive east of the Hof located a beautiful ice lagoon Jokulsarlon. Turn left immediately after the bridge and after a few yards you can rent a boat. Sail between icebergs, reach to the foot of the largest glacier in Iceland whose name is difficult to pronounce by first time: Vatnajokulsthjodgardur.

To get on the black volcanic sand beach, just over the bridge turn to the right. (Diamond, crystal, adamant Beach)

After walking on the South coast, drive another 50 miles East to the town of Hofn. Stay here for the night.

DAY THREE. From Hofn to Egilsstadir with a stop in Stokksnes and Hengifoss. (130 miles in transit).

10 miles East of Hofn is the beautiful black beach of Stokksnes, to get to the beach, traveling 7 miles after Hofn turn from the main road number 1 to the right and go a couple of miles. You're at the place.

After that, head North to Egilsstadir (120 miles) this very scenic spots, the largest fjord in the island's interior is located here.

If you want to walk on foot to places untouched by man, drive 20 miles inland to Hengifoss you will see a spectacular gorge, the origins of the fjord and pristine nature.

After this nature walk you will have strength only for just to go to sleep in Egilsstadir.

DAY FOUR. From Egilsstadir to Akureyri with a view of the lake Myvatn, Dettifoss and Godafoss waterfalls (215 miles in transit).

Continue to travel to the North of the island, going 100 miles to the largest waterfall, Dettifoss. An exciting experience is guaranteed.

After admiring the falls continue your journey, go 50 miles in the direction of Akureyri and stop at the wonderful lake Myvatn. You are in the geothermal area of Namaskard, there are many mud baths. Make a circle around the lake, staying along the way you will be able to walk on the frozen lava.

Continue your way North about 30 miles after lake Myvatn, turn left from the main road to see the waterfall Godafoss.

After such an eventful day trip you will drive another 35 miles to stay overnight in the Akureyri area.

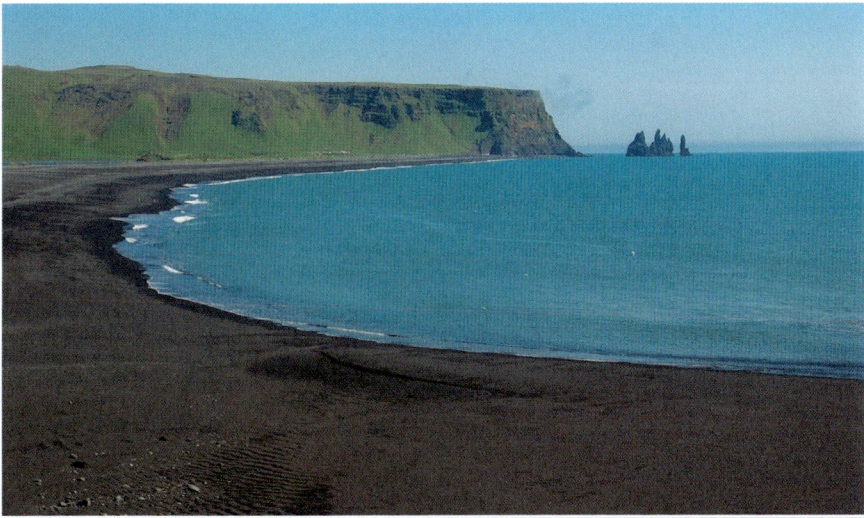

DAY FIVE. Sail through the fjords Akureyri, traveling the North coast, with a stop in Saudarkrokur.

Eat a good Breakfast and head to the Eyjafjordur fjord, at the mouth of Akureyri.

Here you can rent a boat with an experienced captain, and go whale watching. Typically, these tours last up to three hours.

After the tour, drive along the North coast and enjoy the beauty of the Northern fjords. Go with Akureyri from the West take 82 road and continue on the 76 road. You will find 100 miles of beautiful scenic places in the North of Iceland.

Finish your day trip staying in the village of Saudarkrokur.

DAY SIX. From Saudarkrokur to Reykjavík with a view the Deildartunguhver geothermal source, Historical place Reykholt, Hraunfossar and Barnafoss waterfalls (225 miles in transit).

Leave early and drive towards Reykjavik. The first stop will be near 135 miles through the most powerful geothermal spring in Europe Deildartunguhver. This place is recognized as one of the best places to stay in 2016.

4 miles West of Deildartunguhver located the historical place of Reykholt. In this place was the seam of the American and Eurasian tectonic plates.

Then continue the journey inland to the West for another 10 miles. You will come to two wonderful waterfalls Hraunfossar & Barnafoss. These waterfalls spewing huge amounts of water from fields of lava. It is a unbelievable sight.

After that, head to the end point of this trip to the capital Reykjavik. The distance from here to Reykjavik is 75 miles.

On arrival in Reykjavik this trip is over, you can relax in the capital and go elsewhere for new experiences.

CHAPTER 7. HELPFUL INFORMATION TO THE TOURISTS

The official exchange rate is 1$ about to 125 ISK

VISA INFORMATION

Iceland is a party to the Schengen Agreement. This means that U.S. citizens may enter Iceland without a visa for up to 90 days for tourist or business purposes.

Your passport should be valid for at least three months beyond your intended date of departure from the Schengen area.

You need sufficient funds and a backward airline ticket.

If your passport does not meet the Schengen requirements, you may be refused boarding by the airline at your point of origin or while transferring planes. You could also be denied entry when you arrive in the Schengen area. For this reason, we recommend that your passport have at least six months' validity remaining whenever you travel abroad.

If necessary, you can always find support in the Embassy of US in Iceland

USEFUL PHONE NUMBERS

Emergency number 112

Police 444-2500 (with country code +354-444-2500)

Medical assistance 1770

Dental emergency 575-0505

Directory enquiries 1818, 1819 or 1800

MOBILE & INTERNET IN ICELAND

Iceland GSM services (Siminn, Vodafone, TAL and Nova) cover most of the Island, including a large proportion of the unpopulated area of the country. You can always easily buy a prepaid service (phone cards) from any of these GSM operators. At most gas stations or stores in Iceland you can purchase credit refill cards.

Also you can rent a portable WiFi mobile internet hotspot and be connected to the internet anywhere in Iceland.

Unlimited 4G for 10$ a day

How call to Iceland from abroad. Dial:

Landline: **011** (Exit code for USA) **354** (Iceland Code) **4 or 5** (Area Code) **- receiver number**

Cellular: **011** (Exit code for USA) **354** (Iceland Code) **7 Digits Cellular Number**

<u>Iceland area codes usually have 1 digits.</u>

Area Name: *Reykjavik, Area code: 5*

Area Name: *outside Reykjavik, Area code: 4*

Also calls can be made by dialing 00 next the country code and next the telephone number you wish to reach.

THE END

Links

Iceland weather site
http://www.vedur.is

Exchange rate in Iceland
http://www.cb.is/statistics/offical-exchange-rate/

Book air tickets
http://www.icelandair.com/
http://wowair.com/
http://www.delta.com/
http://www.easyjet.com/en

Book ferry to Iceland
http://www.smyrilline.com/

Embassy of US in Iceland
http://iceland.usembassy.gov/

Bus transfers from the Keflavik International Airport:
https://airportexpress.is/
https://www.re.is/flybus/

Order a bus card
http://www.straeto.is/english/buy-tickets/

Rent car in Iceland
http://www.rentalcars.com/en/country/is/
http://www.reykjavikrentacar.is/

Iceland guides
http://www.icelandguide.is/

Reykjavik city card
http://www.visitreykjavik.is/travel/reykjavik-city-card

Accommodation:
Camping's
In the southwestern part of Iceland http://istay.is/campsite/
In the most southern place in Iceland
http://www.vikcamping.is/
In the East of Iceland http://en.visitfjardabyggd.is/where-to-stay/camping/details/Mjoifjordur8
In the North of Iceland http://lonsa.is/en/

Hostel's
In the Reykjavik
https://www.facebook.com/Reykjavik.City.Hostel/
In the South http://www.hostel.is/Hostels/Vik
In the East http://www.hostel.is/Hostels/Seydisfjordur/
In the North http://www.hostel.is/Hostels/Akureyri/

Guest House's
In the Reykjavik http://lily.is/
In the South http://www.likevik.is/
In the East http://www.eyjolfsstadir.is/english
In the North http://www.skjaldarvik.is/

Hotel's
A network of hotels located throughout the island
http://www.hoteledda.is/

Whale watching
https://www.gentlegiants.is/
Northern lights viewing tours
https://www.extremeiceland.is/en/northern-lights-tours-iceland
https://www.extremeiceland.is/en/northern-lights-tours-iceland/magical-auroras

The geothermal beach Nautholsvik
http://nautholsvik.is/desktopdefault.aspx/tabid-716/

Photography Museum of Reykjavik
http://www.visitreykjavik.is/

Lake Ellidavatn
http://gofishing.is/lake-ellidavatn/

Fjord Hvalfjordur
https://www.extremeiceland.is/en/information/about-iceland/hvalfjordur-and-glymur-waterfall

Thingvellir national park
http://www.thingvellir.is/english.aspx

Geothermal Spa Center Blue Lagoon
http://www.bluelagoon.com/

The Great Geysir
https://www.extremeiceland.is/en/information/about-iceland/geysir-geothermal-field

The Peace Tower

http://www.visitreykjavik.is/imagine-peace-tower

Concert hall Harpa
http://en.harpa.is/

Zoological family park
http://reykjavik.is/en/family-park-and-zoo

The Hofdi house
http://www.visitreykjavik.is/hofdi-house

Vikin maritime museum
http://www.visitreykjavik.is/vikin-reykjavik-maritime-museum

The Icelandic phallus Museum
http://www.visitreykjavik.is/icelandic-phallological-museum

Markets in Iceland:
Kolaportid market
http://kolaportid.is/Index.aspx

Kronan markets
https://kronan.is/

Bonus markets
http://www.bonus.is/

Useful phone numbers and websites:
Emergency 112
http://safetravel.is/112-iceland-app/

Police 444-2500 (with country code +354-444-2500)
http://www.logreglan.is/english/

Medical assistance 1770
http://www.sjukra.is/english

Dental emergency 575-0505
http://www.tannlaeknavaktin.is/index.php/in-english

Iceland GSM services
https://www.siminn.is/english/
https://vodafone.is/english
https://www.tal.is/
https://www.nova.is/afylling/en

Unlimited 4G for 10$ a day
http://iceland.trawire.com/

Thanks!

Lars K. Jonsson

Printed in Great Britain
by Amazon